Transfer and Stitch

Romantic Motifs

OVER **60** REUSABLE MOTIFS TO IRON ON AND EMBROIDER

Carina Envoldsen-Harris

SEARCH PRESS

First published in 2016

Search Press Limited
Wellwood, North Farm Road,
Tunbridge Wells, Kent TN2 3DR

Text copyright © Carina Envoldsen-Harris 2016

Illustrations by Bess Harding: pages 9–13

Illustrations by Carina Envoldsen-Harris: transfer sheets 12, 14, 15, 20, 21, 27 (top right, centre right, bottom right), 29

Photographs by Paul Bricknell at Search Press Studios

Photographs and design copyright
© Search Press Ltd, 2016

ISBN: 978-1-78221-295-9

The Publishers and author can accept no responsibility for any consequences arising from the information, advice or instructions given in this publication.

Readers are permitted to reproduce any of the transfers or embroideries in this book for their personal use, or for the purpose of selling for charity, free of charge and without the prior permission of the Publishers. Any use of the tracings or embroideries for commercial purposes is not permitted without the prior permission of the Publishers.

Suppliers
All of the threads used in the book were kindly supplied by DMC Creative World. Visit www.dmc.com for details of your nearest stockist. If you have any difficulty obtaining any of the materials and equipment mentioned in this book, please visit the Search Press website: www.searchpress.com

Publisher's notes
All the embroideries in this book were made by the author, Carina Envoldsen-Harris, using threads supplied by DMC.

Please note: to remove the transfers you want to use from the book, cut round them carefully. They can be stored in the pocket at the back of the book and used several times.

Printed in China

Some of the images used in this book were previously published by Search Press in:

Design Source Book: Art Nouveau Designs by Judy Balchin: transfer sheets 10 (bottom), 17 (top), 19, 22 (right), 25 (left), 26 (top), 27 (right), 30 (top), 32 (top)

Design Source Book: Art Nouveau Flowers by Elaine Hamer: transfer sheets 10 (top), 31

Design Source Book: Flower Designs by Mandy Southan: transfer sheet 1 (bottom)

Design Source Book: Wedding Designs by Sonia Griffin: transfer sheets 1 (top), 3, 5, 26 (bottom)

The Design Library: Art Nouveau Flower Designs by Polly Pinder: transfer sheets 11, 17 (bottom left and bottom right), 22 (left), 23 (top), 24

The Design Library: Flower Designs by Judy Balchin: transfer sheets 2, 4, 9, 16, 18, 28, 30 (bottom)

The Design Library: Heart & Flower Designs by Judy Balchin: transfer sheets 6, 7, 8, 13, 23 (bottom), 25 (right), 32 (bottom)

Dedication
For Tony: thank you for putting up with all the thread and fabric!

Acknowledgements
I would like to thank everyone who helped make this book possible.

To Cara at DMC UK for providing all the beautiful threads for the book.

Thank you to Becky Shackleton, Katie French and everyone else at Search Press.

To my wonderful agent, Kate McKean, huge thanks!

The following have been of great help and kept me sane in the process:
Polly, Christine, Lisa, Marie, Missy and Rebecca - you guys are the best!

To my fellow &Stitches members for putting up with my absence.

And last but not least to my mother, for her expert sewing help.

CONTENTS

Introduction

The art of embroidery has been used for thousands of years as a practical means of joining together, mending and decorating cloth. The basic stitches and techniques are as old as the art itself but these days we also enjoy a variety of materials and colours that stitchers of earlier times could only dream of.

In this book you will find a collection of sixty-three motifs. All the motifs are provided as transfers at the back of the book, and all have been stitched as samplers, on pages 16–81. If you are new to embroidery, have a look through the sections at the start of the book where you will find instructions for the eleven stitches used in the samplers. You will also find tips for choosing materials, transferring motifs and using an embroidery hoop. You may find it useful to practise stitches that are new to you on a separate piece of fabric before you dive into a project.

With each sampler you will find notes on the colours and stitches used, but they are only there as inspiration – don't be afraid to experiment and pick your own colour and stitch combinations. On pages 82–95 are ideas for how you can use the motifs to decorate or personalise textiles with your stitching – I chose to embellish a range of twelve items including a denim pillow cover, a table runner and a dress for a little girl.

I hope you will enjoy the time spent stitching these motifs as well as the end result, whether you are making for yourself or for someone else.

Happy stitching!

Carina +

What you need

You don't need a lot to get started with embroidery – gather
together some fabric, thread, needles, an embroidery hoop and
a pair of scissors and you have all you need.

Fabric

The samplers in the book are stitched on white cotton fabric but you can embroider on pretty much anything you can push a needle through, even paper, card or wood. The projects are stitched on a variety of textiles: cotton, denim and linen. When choosing your fabric, bear in mind that not all fabrics work well with the transfers because of the texture of the fabric or the colour of it. For the best result, use a light-coloured even-weave fabric such as cotton or cotton/linen.

Thread

DMC stranded cotton has been used for the samplers. It comes in a wide range of colours and is colourfast. It can be divided into strands so that the thickness can be adjusted to suit your fabric. Use thicker thread with heavy or textured fabrics, otherwise the stitches may disappear into the weave of the fabric. Other brands of thread are available, as well as other types of thread. Silk, perlé cotton, crewel wool or sashiko thread, for example, all produce interesting results. Even yarn for knitting and crochet can be used. Experiment to see what you like.

Scissors

Three types of scissors are good to have on hand: small sharp embroidery scissors for cutting threads, dressmaking shears for cutting fabric and craft scissors for cutting the transfers. Never use embroidery or fabric scissors to cut paper – it will quickly blunt them.

Needles

For most embroidery, the best needles to use are embroidery/crewel needles. They are fine, sharp needles with a large eye. They range in size from 1–10: the higher the number, the finer the needle. As a general rule, use the higher numbers on finer fabrics, where you will usually use a finer thread, and lower numbers for heavier fabrics. Chenille needles are useful for thick threads and milliner's needles are handy when working a lot of French knots.

Embroidery hoop

An embroidery hoop (sometimes referred to as an embroidery frame) keeps the fabric taut so that your stitches will be more even and prevents the fabric from puckering too much. Hoops are usually wooden, but are also available in plastic. They come in a range of sizes, numbered by their diameter in inches. Use a hoop that is 2.5–5cm (1–2in) larger all around than the motif so you won't have to reposition the hoop. Always take the fabric out of the hoop when you know you will not be working on it for a while. Leaving the fabric in the hoop may create permanent marks on the fabric.

Stitches used

Eleven simple embroidery stitches have been used to produce all of the designs in this book. Don't be afraid to experiment and try different combinations of stitches, thread colours and fabrics – you will be amazed by their versatility and the wonderful effects you can achieve.

Starting to stitch

Bring your needle and thread up through the fabric on the spot where you are going to place your first stitch. You will need to hold the end of the thread to stop it going right through (1). Make sure your first three or four stitches go over the starting thread on the wrong side of the fabric to secure it (2).

Alternatively, make a small knot at the end of your thread and insert the needle down into the fabric about 2.5cm (1in) away from where your first stitch will be placed. It must be along the line of your first few stitches. Bring the needle up where you are going to start stitching (3). Embroider the first few stitches up to the knot, making sure you have stitched over the starting thread on the back of your work. You can now snip off the knot and continue stitching (4).

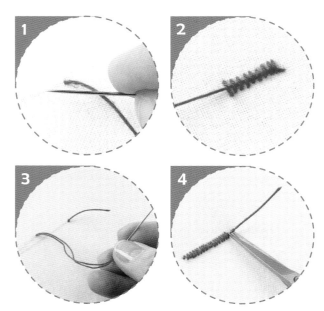

Fastening off a thread

To fasten off a thread, slip the needle through the back of the stitches you have just worked (5), pull the thread through and snip off the tail (6). To rejoin a thread, slip the thread through the back of the same stitches and continue stitching.

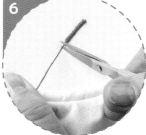

Running stitch

This is the simplest of all the stitches and is great for adding little details. This stitch can be used to outline, add subtle shading, create fine detail, or as the foundation for other stitches.

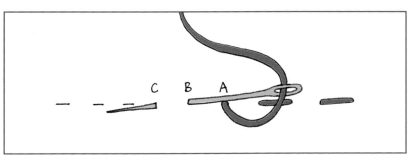

Bring the needle up at A, insert it at B and bring it up again at C. Continue along the stitch line, leaving an equal space between the stitches.

Cross stitch

This simple but effective stitch can be used to outline shapes, to fill areas or singly, for decoration.

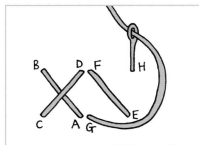

Bring the needle up at A and insert it at B to create one half of your cross. Bring the needle up at C again and then take it down at D to complete.

Backstitch

Backstitch can be used for both curved and straight lines. It is the easiest stitch to use for outlining a shape and is less heavy than chain stitch or stem stitch.

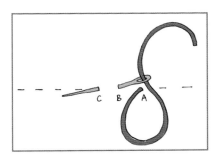

1 Bring the needle up at A and pull the thread through. Insert the needle at B and bring it through at C. Pull the thread through the fabric.

2 Insert the needle at D and bring it up at E. Pull the thread through.

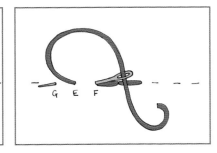

3 Insert the needle at F and bring it up at G. Continue working along the stitch line until it is completed. To finish off, thread your needle through the stitches on the wrong side of your work.

French knots

French knots can be worked singly or in clusters. They are very useful for creating a pretty textured effect within a shape – they are particularly good for creating flower centres.

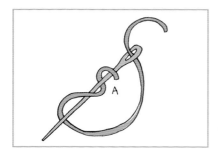
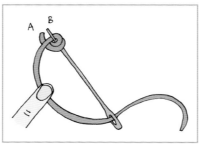
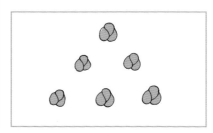

1 Bring the thread through where the knot is required, at A. Holding the thread between your thumb and finger, wrap it around the needle twice.

2 Hold the thread firmly with your thumb and turn the needle back to A. Insert it as close to A as possible, at B, and pull the thread through to form a knot.

3 Make as many knots as you need. Make a small stitch on the wrong side of the fabric before fastening off.

Pistil stitch

This quirky stitch is ideal in floral embroideries for forming the anthers of flowers. However, it could also be used in a more abstract way, and can make a wonderful decorative addition.

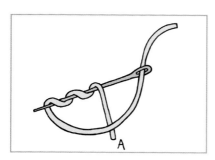
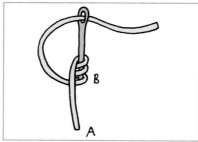
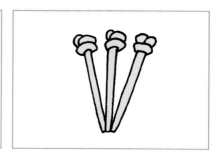

1 Bring the thread through where the knot is required, at A. Holding the thread between your thumb and finger, wrap it around the needle two or three times.

2 Keeping a good tension on the thread, take the needle down at point B, and pull the thread through to form a knot with a 'tail'.

3 Make as many pistil stitches as you need. Make a small stitch on the wrong side of the fabric before fastening off.

Lazy daisy (detached chain) stitch

Lazy daisy is an easy little stitch used to create a sweet daisy design. It can also be used to fill a space when a bolder effect is required – just group some daisy stitches together and then repeat over an area.

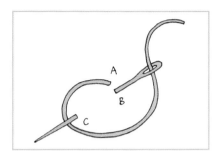

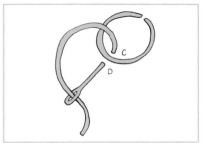

1 Bring the thread through at A and, securing the thread with your thumb, insert the needle at B, as close to A as possible. Bring the needle through at C. Pull the thread through gently to create a loop.

2 Insert the needle at D, making sure you pass the thread over the loop, to secure.

3 Make as many stitches as required, then make a small stitch on the wrong side of your work to secure.

Stem stitch

Stem stitch makes a lovely smooth, unbroken line. It can be worked as an outline stitch or as a filling stitch, when rows are laid down close together. As the name suggests, it is particularly effective when worked along the stems of flowers and plants.

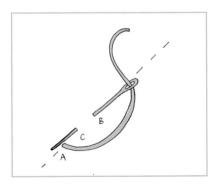

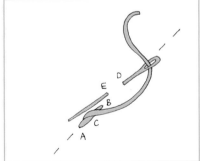

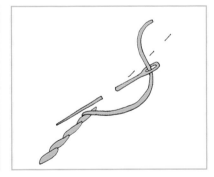

1 Bring the thread through at A and hold it down with your thumb to form a loop. Insert the needle at B and bring it out at C, between A and B.

2 Pull the thread through to make the first stitch. Hold the working thread down with your thumb as before. Insert the needle at D and bring it out at E, slightly to the side of B.

3 Continue until the line of stitching is complete. If using as a filling stitch, simply work another row next to the first and repeat until the area is filled.

Seed stitch

This is a great little stitch. Work it sparsely to give a light shading effect or work lots of overlapping stitches for a great filler. The stitches themselves can be placed at different angles to create a random effect or can be worked in one direction.

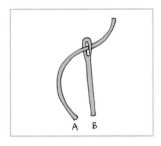

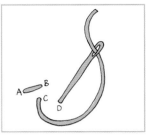

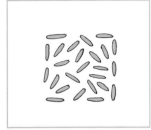

1 Bring the needle up at A and insert it at B to create a tiny stitch.

2 Bring the needle up at C and insert it at D to make a second stitch at a different angle.

3 Continue placing the stitches randomly until the area is filled.

Long and short stitch

Long and short stitch is perfect for filling in larger areas, particularly where a shaded effect is required. You can adjust the length of the stitches to fit the shape you are filling and you can vary the effect with the number of threads used.

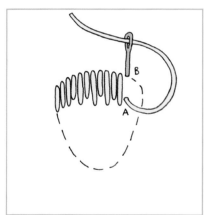

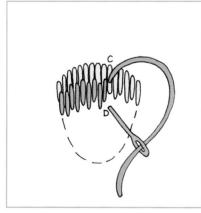

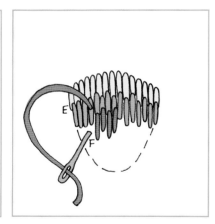

1 Work from the middle of the outer edge of the shape to be filled and move to the left, then come back to the middle and work the right-hand side of the shape. Bring the needle out at A and in at B. Repeat to fill the top edge.

2 Work subsequent rows as before but this time bring the needle out through the stitches at C and in at D. This will ensure a nice, flat surface, free of little holes. Each stitch does not have to be split; sometimes it will be necessary to come up between stitches to give a neat, even fill to the shape.

3 Continue for the next row, coming out at E and in at F, until your shape is completely filled. Remember to vary the stitch lengths to give a smooth, blended finish.

Satin stitch

Satin stitch is good for filling small areas quickly. The stitches look best worked closely together and the effect can be particularly pleasing if a variegated thread is used. By adjusting the length of the stitches it can be worked to fit most shapes. Take care when placing your needle so that you get an even edge.

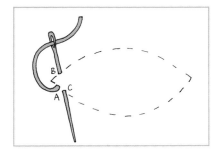
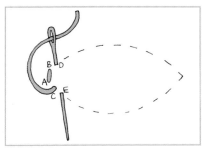
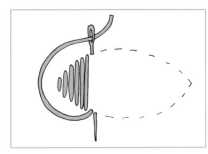

1 Bring your thread up at A, on the edge of the shape, and insert the needle at B. Pull the thread through gently. Pulling the thread too tightly will cause the fabric to pucker. Bring the needle up at C, working as close to A as possible.

2 Take the needle down at D, as close as possible to B, and bring it back through at E, next to C. Pull the thread through gently to make a stitch that lies next to the first stitch, without overlapping it.

3 Continue as above until the shape is filled. Pass the needle through to the back of the work to fasten off. You may find it easier to work one half of the shape at a time, working from the centre out to each side.

Chain stitch

Chain stitch is a very versatile stitch. It makes a great outlining stitch, and can also be used as a filling stitch, worked either in rows or circles – this is less common but equally effective.

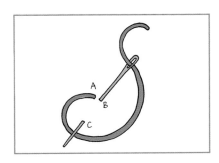
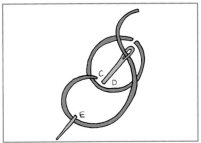
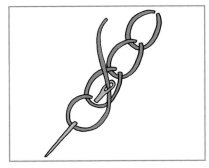

1 Bring the needle up through the fabric at A and pull the thread through. Insert the needle at B, as close as possible to A, and bring it up at C. Keep the thread under the needle. Pull the thread through gently to form the first chain.

2 Insert the needle at D, as close as possible to C, and bring the needle up at E. Keeping the thread under the needle, pull the thread through gently to form the second chain.

3 Continue in this way, making evenly sized chain stitches, until the line of stitching is complete.

Transferring the designs

The transfer sheets for all the designs are at the back of the book (see page 96). You can cut around the parts you want to use individually, but make sure you leave as much paper as possible around the edge. When you have used the transfer, store it in the pocket on the back cover to keep it safe until you wish to use it again. Transfer the designs using an ordinary iron (without steam) set on 'cotton'. Make sure you use a fabric that won't be damaged by this heat. If possible, use a spare piece of your fabric to check before you start.

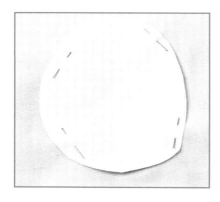

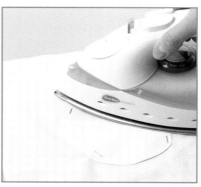

1 Pin the transfer ink-side down on the right side of the fabric where you want the design to be.

2 Place the iron over the transfer area and leave for about ten seconds. Do not move the iron, as this may blur the image. Carefully lift a corner of the transfer to make sure it has printed on to the fabric. If not, leave the iron for a little longer or increase the temperature and try again.

3 When you are happy that the design has transferred successfully, remove the transfer. Your design is now ready to be placed in the embroidery hoop for stitching.

Using dark and heavily patterned fabrics

If your fabric is dark or has a heavy all-over pattern, it may be hard to see the transferred outline. To overcome this problem, embroider the design on to a piece of plain or lighter-coloured fabric and then sew it on to the darker fabric. Alternatively, the transfer can be ironed on to a water-soluble fabric. This can then be tacked (basted) on to the item to be stitched and washed away when the stitching has been completed.

Using an embroidery hoop

If you decide to use an embroidery hoop, make sure it is large enough to include the whole of the design within the frame, but not so large that there is insufficient fabric around the outside to secure it. Binding the inner hoop will not only help to hold the fabric more firmly but also help to prevent the frame marking the fabric. Use a woven tape 2.5cm (1in) wide.

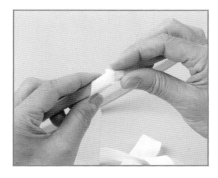

1 Tape the end of the binding at a 45-degree angle. Secure the end with a little piece of masking tape.

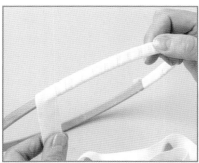

2 Wrap the woven tape around the hoop with one hand whilst using your thumb on the other hand to keep the tape secure. You need to pull the tape fairly tight to stop it sagging and to prevent any gaps appearing.

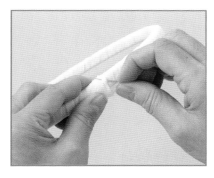

3 When you get back to the start, remove the masking tape and wrap the remaining woven tape over the gap – wrap it a couple of times around the frame, to make sure the ends overlap. Stitch the ends together and trim off any surplus.

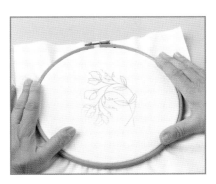

4 Lay the bound inner hoop on a flat surface. Place the fabric over the hoop with the design facing upwards. Keeping the tension screw at the top, put the outer ring over the top and press down to sandwich the fabric between the inner and outer hoops.

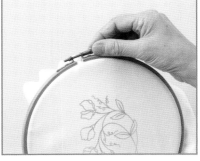

5 Tighten the tension screw: a small screwdriver may be useful.

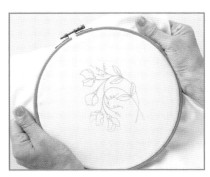

6 Holding the hoop in one hand, gently ease out any slack in the fabric. The fabric should now be drum-tight in the frame.

The samplers

The following stitched samplers, all worked on plain white cotton, give just one idea for stitching each of the designs. Some have been filled in completely with stitch, some have been simply outlined, and others use a combination of the two. Each of the samplers has a corresponding transfer sheet, and is accompanied by notes on the stitches, thread colours and the number of strands used, including the DMC colour codes. This will allow you to reproduce the designs exactly as shown – using either DMC threads or any suitable alternatives – but of course you can also use the samplers as inspiration and create your own embroideries by simply changing the stitches and colours used. You may wish to stitch only a specific part of a design rather than the whole image, in which case just trim the transfer to suit your requirements. When stitching a larger piece, it may be useful to work a small sample on a scrap of waste fabric to check if your colour and stitch choices are working together well.

Getting started

Once you have selected your design, transfer it to your fabric (see page 14) and secure it in an embroidery hoop (see page 15). You are then ready to start. Begin by gathering together the tools and threads you need (see pages 6–7), then select which stitch you want to start with. Start in the centre of the design and work outwards, as this will give a neater finish. Follow the printed lines closely and make sure they are covered as much as possible by the stitching. Although they will fade with washing, they may not disappear completely.

Try to keep the length of the thread you use to approximately 45cm (18in). If the thread twists while you are stitching, try holding your work upside down in the hoop so that the weight of the needle unravels the twist.

Note that the thread numbers provided refer to the DMC threads used; 'var' after the number means it is a variegated (or 'colour variation') thread. Where a variegated thread has been used, you will obtain a slightly different shading effect from the one shown in the picture.

1

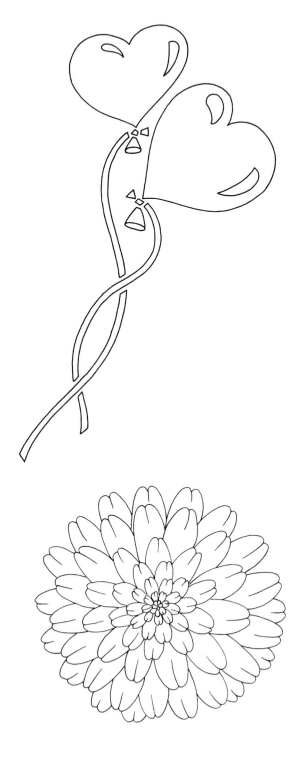

Thread key

DMC colours used:

⬛	3843
⬛	3845
⬜	747
⬜	972
⬛	4200 (var)

Stitches and threads used for the heart-shaped balloons:

⬛ Balloon on the left outlined with backstitch using two strands of 3843.

⬛ Reflections worked in satin stitch using two strands of 3843.

⬛ Balloon on the right outlined with backstitch using two strands of 3845.

⬛ Reflections worked in satin stitch using two strands of 3845.

⬜ Strings outlined with backstitch using two strands of 747.

Stitches and threads used for the flower:

⬜ Centre worked with lazy daisy stitches using two strands of 972.

⬜ Select inner petals worked with backstitch using two strands of 972.

⬛ Remaining petals outlined with backstitch using two strands of 4200 (var).

2

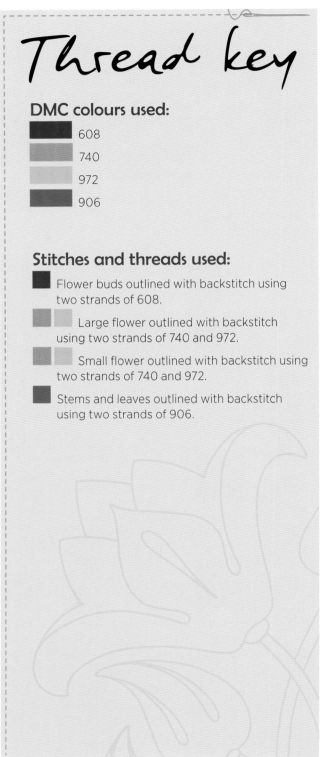

Thread key

DMC colours used:

■	608
■	740
■	972
■	906

Stitches and threads used:

■ Flower buds outlined with backstitch using two strands of 608.

■ ■ Large flower outlined with backstitch using two strands of 740 and 972.

■ ■ Small flower outlined with backstitch using two strands of 740 and 972.

■ Stems and leaves outlined with backstitch using two strands of 906.

3

Thread key

DMC colours used:

964   899

957   955

Stitches and threads used for the top left heart:

Heart outlined with stem stitch using two strands of 964.

Stripes in heart worked in backstitch with two strands of alternating 957, 899 and 955.

Other half of heart outlined in running stitch using two strands of 957.

Stitches and threads used for the bottom right heart:

Heart outlined with chain stitch using two strands of 955.

Small inner heart worked in cross stitch using two strands of 957.

Stitches and threads used for the heart in square:

Large square outlined with backstitch using two strands of 899.

Small inner square outlined with running stitch using two strands of 964.

Large heart outlined with backstitch using two strands of 957.

Middle heart outlined with running stitch using two strands of 955.

Smallest heart outlined with backstitch using two strands of 899.

Cross in centre is a cross stitch worked with two strands of 957.

Stitches and threads used for the horseshoes:

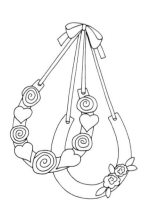

Horseshoes outlined with backstitch using two strands of 964.

Ribbons outlined with stem stitch using two strands of 955.

Hearts outlined with backstitch using two strands of 899.

Spirals outlined with backstitch using two strands of 957.

Leaves outlined with backstitch using two strands of 955.

Flowers outlined with backstitch using two strands of 957 and 899.

4

Thread key

DMC colours used:

▬	3820
▬	4180 (var)
▬	972
▬	741
▬	988
▬	3819

Stitches and threads used for the poppies:

Border worked in chain stitch using two strands of 3820.

Flowers outlined in backstitch using two strands of 4180 (var).

Centre circle outlined in backstitch using two strands of 972.

Anthers worked in lazy daisy stitch using two strands of 741.

Flower buds and stems outlined with two strands of 988.

Pointed leaves outlined with two strands of 3819.

5

Thread key

DMC colours used:

■	3705
■	959
■	4110 (var)
■	4060 (var)

Stitches and threads used for the left-hand dove:

■ Dove outlined with stem stitch using two strands of 3705.

■ Eye worked in satin stitch using two strands of 959.

■ Ribbon worked in satin stitch using two strands of 4110 (var).

Stitches and threads used for the right-hand dove:

■ Dove outlined with stem stitch using two strands of 959.

■ Eye worked in satin stitch using two strands of 3705.

■ Ribbon worked in satin stitch using two strands of 4060 (var).

6

Thread key

DMC colours used:

	3841
	995
	996
	741
	740
	608

Stitches and threads used:

Scalloped edge outlined with stem stitch using two strands of 3841.

Stems worked in stem stitch using two strands of 995.

Leaves worked in lazy daisy stitch using two strands of 996.

Large flowers outlined with backstitch using two strands of 741, with centres worked in satin stitch using two strands of 741.

Remaining flowers outlined with backstitch using two strands of 740 or 608, and centres worked in satin stitch using two strands of 740 or 608.

7

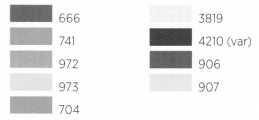

Thread key

DMC colours used:

▮	666	▯	3819
▮	741	▮	4210 (var)
▮	972	▮	906
▯	973	▯	907
▮	704		

Stitches and threads used for the left-hand flower:

▮ Hearts outlined with backstitch using two strands of 666.

▮ Dots worked in French knots using two strands of 666.

▮ ▮ ▯ Petals worked in long and short stitch, using two strands of 741, 972 and 973, starting with 741 at the centre.

▮ Small leaves worked in satin stitch using two strands of 704.

▯ Large leaves outlined with stem stitch using two strands of 3819.

▯ Stem outlined with stem stitch using two strands of 3819.

Stitches and threads used for the right-hand flower:

▮ Centres of flowers worked in satin stitch using two strands of 666.

▮ Solid colour on petals worked in long and short stitch using two strands of 4210 (var).

▮ Petals outlined in stem stitch using two strands of 741.

▮ ▯ ▯ Leaves worked in long and short stitch, using two strands of 906, 907 and 3819, starting with 906 at the pointed end.

▯ Stem outlined with stem stitch using two strands of 907.

8

Thread key

DMC colours used:

■	956
▢	3846
■	3844
■	995

Stitches and threads used:

■ Hearts outlined in backstitch using two strands of 956.

▢ Stripes from large hearts outlined in backstitch using two strands of 3846.

■ Birds, wings and tails outlined in backstitch using two strands of 3844.

■ Eyes of birds outlined in backstitch using two strands of 956.

▢ Tree trunk and branches outlined in backstitch using two strands of 3846.

■ Small leaves inside tree outlined in backstitch using two strands of 995.

■ Large leaves above hearts outlined in backstitch using two strands of 995.

■ Small leaves outlined in backstitch using two strands of 3844.

■ Small hearts on tree outlined in backstitch using two strands of 3844.

▢ Stripes behind birds outlined in backstitch using two strands of 3846.

■ Stripes above birds outlined in backstitch using two strands of 956.

■ Half circles at the bottom outlined in backstitch using two strands of 995.

▢ Stripes by half circles at the bottom outlined in backstitch using two strands of 3846.

9

Thread key

DMC colours used:

▭	4100 (var)
▭	988
▭	3689
▭	603
▭	3805

Stitches and threads used:

Rose and rose bud outlined in stem stitch using two strands of 4100 (var).

Leaves outlined in stem stitch using two strands of 988.

Stems worked in satin stitch using two strands of 988.

The two nearest sections of ribbon worked with French knots using three strands of 3689. Two skeins of 3689 are needed.

The middle left section of ribbon worked with French knots using two strands of 603.

The back sections of ribbon worked in long and short stitch using two strands of 3805.

10

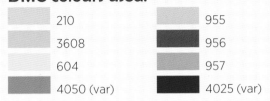

Thread key

DMC colours used:

	210			955
	3608			956
	604			957
	4050 (var)			4025 (var)

Stitches and threads used for the top embroidery:

Top roses outlined with stem stitch using two strands of 210, 3608 and 604 working clockwise from the top.

Heart-shaped leaves above the roses outlined with stem stitch using two strands of 4050 (var).

Leaves below the roses are outlined with stem stitch using two strands of 955.

Small branches with leaves outlined in stem stitch using two strands of 4050 (var).

Stems and heart-shaped leaves at the bottom outlined in stem stitch using two strands of 955.

Stitches and threads used for the bottom embroidery:

Middle rose worked in satin stitch using two strands of 956.

Other roses worked in satin stitch using two strands of 957.

Leaves outlined in stem stitch using two strands of 4025 (var).

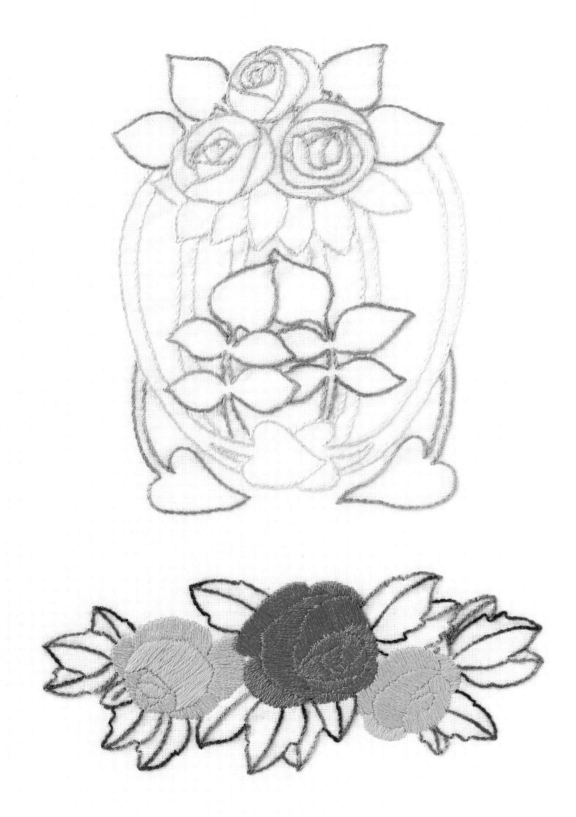

11

Thread key

DMC colours used:

■	4200 (var)	■	4045 (var)
■	728	■	107 (var)
■	3819	■	907

Stitches and threads used for the top embroidery:

■ Four-petal flowers outlined in stem stitch using two strands of 4200 (var).

■ Flower centres outlined with stem stitch using two strands of 728.

■ Anthers worked in pistil stitch using two strands of 728.

■ Pods and stems outlined with backstitch using two strands of 3819.

■ Triangular leaves outlined in backstitch using two strands of 3819.

■ Remaining leaves outlined in backstitch using two strands of 4045 (var).

Stitches and threads used for the bottom embroidery:

■ Tulip flowers worked in satin stitch using two strands of 107 (var).

■ Tulip buds worked in backstitch using two strands of 107 (var).

■ Stems and leaves outlined with backstitch using one strand of 907.

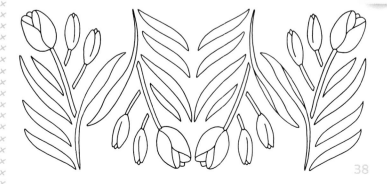

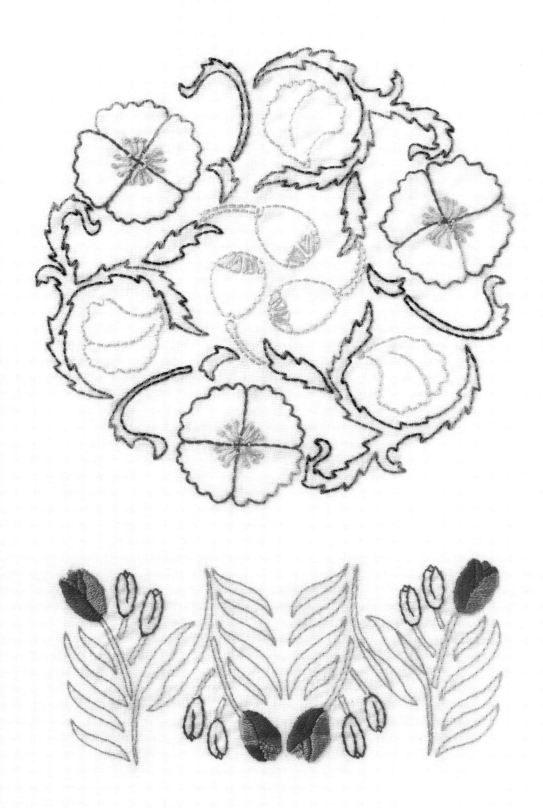

Thread key

DMC colours used:

▇	956	▇▇	3805
▇	973	▢	747
▇	741	▇▇	996
▇	3846	▇	728

Stitches and threads used for the butterfly with heart:

▇ Top part of the wing outlined with stem stitch using two strands of 956.

▇▇▇ Wing markings on the top wing worked in long and short stitch using two strands of 973, 741 and 956, starting from the points of the shapes.

▇ Bottom part of the wing outlined in stem stitch using two strands of 973.

▇▇ Wing markings on the bottom wing worked in long and short stitch using two strands of 956 and 3846, starting from the points of the shapes.

▇ Body and antenna outlined in stem stitch using two strands of 3846. Legs worked as single rows of chain stitch using two strands of 3846.

▇ Outer heart outlined in chain stitch using two strands of 956.

▇ Inner heart outlined in chain stitch using two strands of 741. The space in between the inner and outer hearts is filled with long straight stitches using two strands of 741.

Stitches and threads used for the flying butterfly:

▇ Inner outline of the top wing outlined with chain stitch using two strands of 3805.

▇▇▇ Top wing tips worked in long and short stitch using two strands of 973, 741 and 956, working outwards.

▇ Inner outline of the bottom wing is outlined in chain stitch using two strands of 3846.

▇▇▇ Bottom wing tips are worked in long and short stitch using two strands of 3805, 956 and 741, working outwards.

▇ Body and antenna outlined in stem stitch using two strands of 973.

Stitches and threads used for the ring:

▢ Top of the stone is worked in satin stitch using two strands of 747.

▇▇▇ Angled facets of the stone worked in sections of satin stitch using two strands of 996, 3846 and 3846.

▇▇ Sides of the stone are worked in sections of satin stitch using two strands of 3846, 996 and 747.

▇ Ring band worked in satin stitch using two strands of 728.

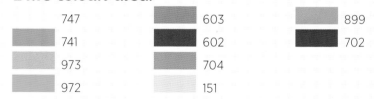

13

Thread key

DMC colours used:

747	603	899
741	602	702
973	704	
972	151	

Stitches and threads used for the heart:

Inner and outer hearts outlined with backstitch using two strands of 747.

Heart filled with straight stitches using two strands of 747.

Bow outlined with stem stitch using one strand of 741 and filled with long and short stitch using two strands of 973 and 972, starting from the bottom of the bow.

Inside of the bow worked in satin stitch using two strands of 741.

Ribbon outlined with stem stitch using one strand of 973 and filled with long and short stitch using two strands of 972.

Flower and buds worked in stem stitch using two strands of 603.

Sprigs worked in stem stitch and French knots using two strands of 602.

Leaves outlined with stem stitch using two strands of 704.

Leaf ribs worked in long straight stitch using two strands of 704.

Stitches and threads used for the flowers:

Flowers outlined with stem stitch using two strands of (top to bottom) 899, 602, 151 and 899.

Flower buds outlined with stem stitch using two strands of (top to bottom, clockwise) 151, 602, 602, 151, 151, 602 and 899.

Six of the leaves outlined in stem stitch using two strands of 704 with leaf ribs worked in long straight stitch with two strands of 704.

Five of the leaves outlined in stem stitch using two strands of 702 with leaf ribs worked in long straight stitch with two strands of 702. The stems are worked in stem stitch using two strands of 702.

Sprigs worked in stem stitch and French knots using two strands of 972.

Small hearts worked in lazy daisy stitch using two strands of 741.

Thread key

DMC colours used:

907	956	210	906
307	891	3608	321
972	3689	3819	988
957	740	996	973

Stitches and threads used for the spring heart (top):

All stems and leaves are outlined in backstitch using two strands of 907.

Daffodil petals outlined in backstitch using two strands of 307. The crown is outlined in backstitch using two strands of 972, with details worked in straight stitch.

Dogwood flower outlined in backstitch using two strands of 957. The darker sections are worked in satin stitch using two strands of 956. The centre is filled with French knots using two strands of 972.

Camellias outlined in backstitch using two strands of 891, with centre details worked in straight stitch using two strands of 307.

Magnolias outlined in backstitch using two strands of 3689. The partial fill is worked in long and short stitch using two strands of 3689 and 957, starting at the bottom.

Tulips outlined in backstitch using two strands of 740.

Stitches and threads used for the summer heart (bottom):

Sweet pea petals outlined in backstitch using two strands of 210 and 3608. The stem and tendrils are outlined in backstitch using two strands of 3819.

Cornflowers outlined in backstitch using two strands of 996. The stem is outlined with backstitch using two strands of 906. The centre is filled with lazy daisy stitch using two strands of 972.

Poppy outlined in backstitch using two strands of 321. The centre is worked in satin stitch using two strands of 3819, surrounded by lazy daisy stitch using two strands of 3819.

Poppy buds outlined in backstitch using two strands of 988, with details of straight stitch in the same colour.

Gladiolus outlined in backstitch using two strands of 956. The details are worked in backstitch using two strands of the same colour. The anthers are worked in pistil stitch using two strands of 973.

Gladiolus buds outlined in backstitch using two strands of 956 and 906.

15

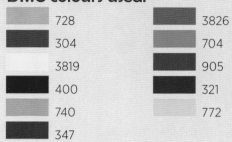

Thread key

DMC colours used:

728		3826	
304		704	
3819		905	
400		321	
740		772	
347			

Stitches and threads used for the autumn heart (top):

All the leaves are outlined in backstitch using two strands of thread. Clockwise from top right: 728, 304, 3819, 400, 740, 347, 3826, 704. All the ribs are stitched in backstitch except the leaf stitched in 347; these ribs are worked in long straight stitch.

Stitches and threads used for the winter heart (bottom):

Holly leaves outlined in backstitch using two strands of 905.

Holly berries worked in satin stitch using two strands of 321.

Mistletoe leaves outlined in backstitch using two strands of 704.

Mistletoe berries worked in satin stitch using two strands of 772, with French knot details using two strands of 704.

16

Thread key

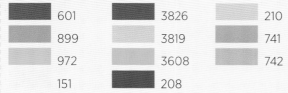

DMC colours used:

601	3826	210
899	3819	741
972	3608	742
151	208	

Stitches and threads used for the top embroidery:

Open blossoms outlined in stem stitch using three strands of 601.

Closed blossoms outlined in stem stitch using two strands of 899.

Anthers worked in pistil stitch using one strand of 972.

Buds outlined in stem stitch using two strands of 151.

Branch worked in satin stitch using two strands of 3826.

Leaves worked in lazy daisy stitch using two strands of 3819.

Stitches and threads used for the bottom embroidery:

Stems worked in stem stitch using three strands of 3608.

Large leaves outlined in chain stitch using two strands of 208.

Small leaves outlined in chain stitch using two strands of 210.

Buds outlined in chain stitch using two strands of 741.

Scalloped edge on flowers is worked in straight stitch using three strands of 742.

Flower circles outlined in chain stitch using two strands of 210.

Flower spokes worked in straight stitch using two strands of 3608. The flower centre ring is outlined in stem stitch using two strands of 3608. The flower centre dot is worked in French knot using two strands of 3608.

17

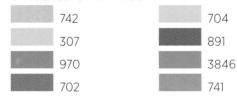

Thread key

DMC colours used:

▨	742	▨	704
▨	307	▨	891
▨	970	▨	3846
▨	702	▨	741

Stitches and threads used for the top embroidery:

▨ ▨ Flower petals worked in satin stitch using two strands of either 742 or 307.

▨ Flower centres worked in satin stitch using two strands of 970.

▨ Stems worked in backstitch using one strand of 702.

▨ ▨ Leaves worked in backstitch using one strand of either 702 or 704.

Stitches and threads used for the bottom-left embroidery:

▨ Petals are worked in satin stitch using two strands of 891.

▨ ▨ Leaves are filled with long and short stitch using two strands of 3846, with details worked in stem stitch using two strands of 891.

Stitches and threads used for the bottom-right embroidery:

▨ Petals are outlined in stem stitch using two strands of 741.

▨ Leaves are outlined in chain stitch using two strands of 3846.

▨ Thorns and stems are outlined in stem stitch using two strands of 3846.

18

Thread key

DMC colours used:

	973		972
	4190 (var)		4180 (var)
	704		3819

Stitches and threads used for the left-hand embroidery:

Petals outlined in stem stitch using two strands of 973.

Dots worked in French knots using two strands of 973.

Flower crown worked in long and short stitch using two strands of 4190 (var).

Flower buds outlined in stem stitch using two strands of 973.

Stems outlined in stem stitch using two strands of 704.

Leaves worked in satin stitch using two strands of 704.

Stitches and threads used for the right-hand embroidery:

Flower centres outlined in chain stitch using two strands of 972.

Flower petals outlined in chain stitch using two strands of 4180 (var).

Flower bud centres outlined in chain stitch using two strands of 4180 (var).

Flower bud petals outlined in chain stitch using two strands of 972.

Leaves and stems outlined in chain stitch using two strands of 3819.

19

Thread key

DMC colours used:

107 (var)

4050 (var)

Stitches and threads used:

Roses outlined in stem stitch using two strands of 107 (var).

Leaves and stems outlined in stem stitch using two strands of 4050 (var).

20

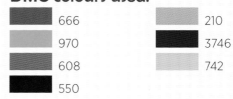

Thread key

DMC colours used:

- 666
- 970
- 608
- 550
- 210
- 3746
- 742

Stitches and threads used for the top embroidery:

Hearts outlined in backstitch using two strands of either 666, 970 or 608.

Birds outlined in backstitch using two strands of 550.

Stitches and threads used for the bottom embroidery:

Dove body worked in satin stitch using two strands of 210.

Dove wings worked in backstitch using two strands of 210.

Dove tail worked in backstitch, with straight stitch details, using two strands of 210.

Dove beak worked in satin stitch using two strands of 550.

Swallow body worked in satin stitch using two strands of 3746.

Swallow wings worked in backstitch with straight stitch details, using two strands of 3746.

Swallow beak worked in satin stitch using two strands of 550.

Ribbons worked in stem stitch using two strands of 970 (left) and 742 (right).

Hearts worked in stem stitch using two strands of 742 (left) and 970 (right).

21

Thread key

DMC colours used:

▢	955	▢	964
▩	603	▢	4180 (var)
▩	210	▢	90 (var)

Stitches and threads used for the butterfly:

Butterfly body and antennae outlined in chain stitch using two strands of 955.

Top wings outlined in chain stitch using two strands of 603.

Bottom wings outlined in chain stitch using two strands of 210.

Wing markings outlined in chain stitch using two strands of 964.

Stitches and threads used for the swans:

Left swan outlined in stem stitch using two strands of 4180 (var) with satin stitch detail in the same colour above the beak.

Right swan outlined in stem stitch using two strands of 90 (var) with satin stitch detail in the same colour above the beak.

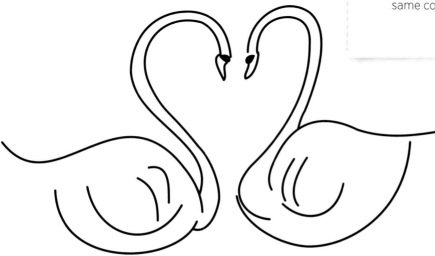

22

Thread key

DMC colours used:

- 704
- 996
- 3746
- 550
- 4200 (var)
- 915

Stitches and threads used for the left-hand embroidery:

- Leaves and stems outlined in stem stitch using two strands of 704.
- Blue petals worked in satin stitch using two strands of 996.
- Lilac petals worked in satin stitch using two strands of 3746.
- Flower centres worked in satin stitch using two strands of 550 (the centre) and 3746 (top and bottom). Straight stitch is used for the details using two strands of 3746.

Stitches and threads used for the right-hand embroidery:

- Twisting stems outlined in backstitch using two strands of 4200 (var).
- Heart-shaped leaves worked in chain stitch using two strands of 915.

23

DMC colours used:

▬ 51 (var)		▬ 961	
▬ 741		▬ 4200 (var)	
▬ 3831			

Stitches and threads used for the top embroidery:

▬ Tips of the tulip petals outlined in backstitch using two strands of 51 (var).

▬ Tulip petals, including details, outlined in backstitch using two strands of 741.

▬ Stems outlined in backstitch using two strands of 3831.

▬ Leaves in the centre outlined in backstitch using two strands of 3831.

▬ Two small leaves at the top outlined in backstitch using two strands of 3831.

▬ Remaining leaves outlined in backstitch using two strands of 961.

Stitches and threads used for the bottom embroidery:

▬ Large hearts outlined in stem stitch using two strands of 741.

▬ Remaining hearts outlined in stem stitch using two strands of 4200 (var).

24

25

Thread key

DMC colours used:

▨	4190 (var)	▨	956
▨	702	▨	604
▨	973	▨	3689

Stitches and threads used for the left-hand embroidery:

▨ Ring worked in satin stitch using two strands of 4190 (var).

Stitches and threads used for the right-hand embroidery:

▨ Leaves and stems outlined in backstitch using two strands of 702.

▨ Small hearts worked in lazy daisy stitch using two strands of 973.

▨ Outer petals on the large flowers worked in satin stitch using two strands of 956.

▨ Remaining petals outlined in stem stitch using two strands of 956.

▨ Outer petals on the medium flowers worked in satin stitch using two strands of 604.

▨ Remaining petals outlined in stem stitch using two strands of 604.

▨ Large and medium flower centres worked in satin stitch using two strands of 973 with details worked in lazy daisy stitch using two strands of 973.

▨ Small flower petals outlined in stem stitch using two strands of 3689.

▨ Small flower centres worked in straight stitch using two strands of 973.

26

Thread key

DMC colours used:

■	4210 (var)	■	728
■	891	■	3845
■	995	■	4050 (var)

Stitches and threads used for the bottom embroidery:

■ Small heart worked in satin stitch using two strands of 4210 (var).

■ Small leaves at the bottom worked in satin stitch using two strands of 891.

■■ Petals worked in long and short stitch using 4210 (var) and 891. Starting with 891 at the centre, alternate the two colours near the centre and the tips.

Stitches and threads used for the peacock:

■ Head and body outlined in stem stitch using two strands of 995.

■ Beak worked in satin stitch using two strands of 728.

■ Small feathers on the head outlined in stem stitch using two strands of 728.

■ Eye worked in satin stitch using two strands of 3845.

■ Short wing feathers outlined in stem stitch with straight stitch details using two strands of 995.

■■■ Medium feathers on the left outlined in stem stitch using two strands of alternating 995 and 3845, with straight stitch in 728 for details.

■■ Medium feathers on the right outlined in stem stitch using two strands of 3845, with straight stitch in 728 for details.

■■ Long wing feathers outlined in stem stitch using two strands of alternating 4050 (var) and 3845.

■ Tail feathers outlined in stem stitch using two strands of 4050 (var) and 728.

27

Thread key

DMC colours used:

■	321	■	208
■	956	■	743
■	741	■	954
■	210	■	907
■	3608		

Stitches and threads used for the heart:

■ Hearts and scalloped edge worked in chain stitch using two strands of 321.

■ Petals in scalloped border worked in lazy daisy stitch using two strands of 956.

■ Stripes in heart filled with seed stitch using two strands of 956.

Stitches and threads used for the top banner:

■ Ribbon outlined in stem stitch using two strands of 741.

Stitches and threads used for the bottom banner:

■ Ribbon outlined in chain stitch using two strands of 956.

Stitches and threads used for the border embroidery:

■ Large flowers worked in satin stitch using two strands of 210.

■ ■ Small flowers worked in satin stitch using two strands of 3608 or 208.

■ Flower centres filled with French knots using two strands of 743.

■ Large leaves outlined in stem stitch using two strands of 954.

■ Small leaves outlined in stem stitch using two strands of 907.

28

Thread key

DMC colours used:

- 4190 (var)
- 106 (var)
- 90 (var)
- 92 (var)

Stitches and threads used for the top embroidery:

Negative space around the flower worked in long and short stitch using two strands of 4190 (var).

Details inside flower and elements that fall outside the circle outlined in stem stitch using two strands of 4190 (var).

Stitches and threads used for the bottom embroidery:

Petals outlined in stem stitch using two strands of 106 (var).

Circle in the centre worked in satin stitch surrounded by lazy daisy stitch using two strands of 90 (var).

Stem and leaves outlined in stem stitch using two strands of 92 (var).

29

Thread key

DMC colours used:

	955
■	3819
	957
■	972
■	704

Stitches and threads used for the single heart:

Left half outlined in stem stitch using two strands of 955.

Right half outlined in stem stitch using two strands of 3819.

Negative space filled with cross stitch using two strands of 957.

Stitches and threads used for the rings:

Rings outlined in stem stitch with straight stitch details using two strands of 972.

Ribbon worked in chain stitch using two strands of 957.

Stitches and threads used for the double hearts:

Left heart outlined in chain stitch using two strands of 3819.

Right heart outlined in chain stitch using two strands of 704.

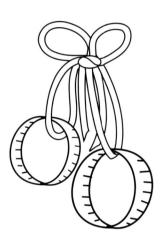

30

Thread key

DMC colours used:

■	601	▢	210
■	3608	■	90 (var)
■	988	■	704
■	956		

Stitches and threads used for the rose:

■ Rose and rose bud outlined in stem stitch using two strands of 601.

■ Rose and rose bud filled with seed stitch using two strands of 3608.

■ Stems and leaves outlined in stem stitch using two strands of 988.

Stitches and threads used for the daisies and tulips:

■ Tulips outlined in stem stitch using two strands of 956.

▢ Daisy petals outlined in stem stitch using two strands of 210.

■ Daisy centres filled with chain stitch, worked in a spiral from the middle, using two strands of 90 (var).

■ Stems and leaves outlined in stem stitch using two strands of 704.

31

Thread key

DMC colours used:

- 106 (var)
- 90 (var)
- 906
- 3819

Stitches and threads used:

Petals outlined in stem stitch using two strands of 106 (var).

Anthers outlined in stem stitch using two strands of 90 (var) with details worked in satin stitch.

Buds outlined in stem stitch using two strands of 906.

Stems and leaves outlined in stem stitch using two strands of 3819.

32

DMC colours used:

■	3826	■	956
■	704	■	996
■	972	■	957
■	741		

Stitches and threads used for the basket:

■ Basket outlined in backstitch using two strands of 3826.

■ Leaves outlined in backstitch using two strands of 704.

■ ■ Petals worked in satin stitch using two strands of either 972 or 741.

■ Flower centres filled with French knots using two strands of 956.

Stitches and threads used for the heart border:

■ Petals worked in long and short stitch using two strands of 996.

■ Flower centres filled with French knots using two strands of 972.

■ ■ Hearts outlined in stem stitch using three strands of either 956 or 957.

■ Frame outlined in backstitch using two strands of 972.

The projects

The projects on the following pages are further inspiration for how you can use the motifs in this book; they use different colours and stitches to the samplers. When choosing fabrics and threads for your projects, it is a good idea to keep the end use in mind. Will the project need frequent washing and ironing, for example? If this is the case, you may want to prewash the fabric to avoid shrinkage after you have embroidered it.

There is a huge variety of fabrics to stitch on, including linen, cotton, denim, felt and even knitted fabrics. Some fabrics, such as jersey or very fine fabrics, may need a stabiliser to make them easy to stitch on. Six-stranded cotton embroidery thread may be the obvious choice for your projects but there are many other types of thread available to experiment with, such as crewel wool, perlé cotton and metallic threads. Even knitting yarn can be used to great effect on heavier fabrics or on items like knitted mittens or sweaters. It may be a good idea to stitch a small sample to test the colour-fastness of the threads you want to use, especially if you are using special or hand-dyed threads. Not all threads stand up to washing, so bear this in mind when making your selection. Metallics or wool, for example, will not work well for items that will need frequent washing, but they can be washed by hand in cold water. Check the guidelines from the manufacturer when using special threads.

Before you start stitching, prepare your fabric by pressing it to get rid of creases. Raw edges can be hemmed or trimmed with pinking shears to reduce fraying. The transfers work best on light-coloured fabrics, but for darker colours you can copy the designs and then use a transfer method that is suitable for your fabric.

Dress

A colourful butterfly makes a lovely decoration on an otherwise plain dress for a little girl. If you enjoy sewing, you could make your own dress, but you can also embroider onto a ready-made dress to give it a personal touch.

Denim pillow

Play with different combinations
of materials to create interesting
textures, as in this denim pillow
stitched with crewel wool.

85

Patchwork pillow

Patchwork and embroidered motifs make
a lovely combination. Why not combine
them in a colourful pillow cover? There
are plenty of possibilities when selecting
different fabrics and colours.

Tea towel

Spice up a tea towel with bright colours, as with this
flower motif. Why not make a set using different
colour combinations and give them as a gift?

Skirt

I have embroidered this skirt with a peacock motif and added extra sparkle by using metallic threads.

Pillowcase

The combination of the white floral motif on a red background gives this pillowcase a Scandinavian feel.

Banner or pennant

A banner or pennant is a fun decoration for a sewing room or a child's bedroom. You could even personalise it with the child's name.

Table runner

Change the colours of a motif to suit the item you are decorating. Use the colours to match the item or to create a contrast – here I have used red stitches to contrast with the blue-grey stripes.

Place mats

Hand-stitched place mats make a beautiful gift. You could embroider the same motif on each of them or choose different motifs but using the same colour scheme.

Shirt

An item of clothing can be transformed with embroidery. Either use a motif in subtle pastel colours like the balloons on this denim shirt, or use a burst of bright colours.

Tablecloth

Make an embroidery the centrepiece of a tablecloth. Smaller elements can be used to embellish the corners.

Apron

Embroidery is an effective way to pull together different elements of an item of clothing: here the flowery motif complements both the floral background and the gingham pocket of this apron.

The transfers

Each of the following transfers corresponds to one of the samplers on pages 16–81 and can be used up to ten times. Remove them from the book by cutting carefully around them with scissors, then store them in the pocket on the back cover. Make sure you leave as much paper as possible around the motif.

Note that the transfer ink will fade from the fabric with washing but may not disappear completely, so when stitching, follow the printed lines as closely as possible to ensure they are hidden beneath the stitching.

2

4

6

8

9

12

14

22

27

28